Inheritance

BarcodeCW00555803

BDO Stoy Hayward specialises in helping businesses, whether start-ups or multinationals, to grow. By working directly with fast-track organisations and the entrepreneurs behind them, we've developed a robust understanding of the factors that govern business growth. BDO Stoy Hayward is a member of the BDO International network, the world's fifth largest accountancy organisation, with representation in more than ninety countries.

Wendy Walton is a partner in BDO Stoy Hayward, where she specialises in providing tax advice to wealthy private individuals, with particular emphasis on trust structures, inheritance tax and international aspects. She is a Chartered Tax Adviser, a Certified Accountant and a member of the Society of Trust and Estate Practitioners. She has written and lectured extensively on various aspects of personal and international taxation. Wendy enjoys spending her leisure time with her young family.

Inheritance Tax Planning

A BDO Stoy Hayward Guide

Wendy Walton

PROFILE BOOKS

First published in Great Britain in 2004 by
PROFILE BOOKS LTD
58A Hatton Garden
London EC1N 8LX
www.profilebooks.co.uk

A CIP catalogue record for this book is available from the British Library.

ISBN 1 86197 756 5

Typeset in Galliard by MacGuru Ltd
info@macguru.org.uk

Printed in Great Britain by
Bookmarque, Croydon, Surrey

While care has been taken to ensure the accuracy of the contents of this book, it is intended to provide general guidance only and does not constitute professional advice.

Contents

Foreword

No one likes paying tax. This is especially true of inheritance tax – it is a tax on the wealth you have built up during your lifetime, on which you have probably already paid income tax or capital gains tax. Inheritance tax is also becoming of increasing concern as property prices rise, pushing many people above the current inheritance tax threshold.

Looking on the bright side, there are lots of valuable exemptions and reliefs available, which means that with proper planning your inheritance tax bill can be minimised. The most valuable exemption states that if you give something away during your lifetime, it is free from inheritance tax provided that you survive for at least seven years after the gift has been made. This requires planning ahead to achieve a sensible balance between minimising the tax for your family while still keeping a comfortable lifestyle for yourself.

However, people often shy away from planning for inheritance tax or writing a will, as facing up to the prospect of death can be very difficult. Another reason for reluctance as far as inheritance tax is concerned is that, although the tax is paid on your wealth, it is the people to whom you leave your assets who actually suffer the tax.

Wendy Walton has many years' experience in advising people how to preserve their family wealth. In this book she outlines the various planning opportunities you can take to ensure that your family will not have to pay unnecessary taxes. Above all, she demonstrates that giving inheritance tax a little thought now can save substantial amounts later on.

JEREMY NEWMAN
Managing Partner
BDO Stoy Hayward

1

Introduction

INHERITANCE TAX (IHT) is a tax due on your death and on certain gifts you make during your lifetime. Most lifetime gifts are exempt from IHT if you survive seven years from the date of the gift – but you have to watch out for other tax implications when making gifts, such as capital gains tax.

IHT can be an expensive tax and a proportion of the wealth that you have worked so hard to accumulate during your lifetime (and paid tax on!) will go to the government rather than your family. It can also trigger strong emotions, particularly if it requires your children to sell the family home in order to pay the tax.

It has often been said that IHT is a voluntary tax – but without careful planning this is unlikely to be the case. If your estate is worth more than £255,000 (for deaths during 2003/04), then tax will be due on the excess at 40%. With increasing property prices, this threshold can soon be met. On an estate of £500,000, tax of almost £100,000 is due. According to Inland Revenue statistics there were only 25,000 taxpayers who suffered IHT in 2002/03. But in actual money terms that equates to an expected total of £2.35 billion in IHT for that year.

IHT is still a political hot potato and there have been numerous threats that amendments will be made to the law by the current government. To date, however, this government has made very little change, so now is an ideal time to review your financial position and consider the planning opportunities available. Failure to do so could lead to disappointment in the future.

This book seeks to give you an introduction to IHT – the planning that is available and the pitfalls to watch out for. One of the first steps in IHT planning is to ensure that you have an up-to-date will. You also need to add up the value of your estate and look at your income and spending. You may wish to make some lifetime gifts or change the mix of your estate, so that some of the assets qualify for IHT exemptions. Alternatively, you may want to think about doing some planning around your family home or setting up a trust for your grand-children.

This book is written as a general guide, starting with the basics, such as the importance of making a will, and going on to more complex tax planning, such as the use of trusts and what can be done with the family home. Wherever possible, I have used examples to help make the position clearer. However, this is not a book about dealing with death, bereavement counselling, or the legalities of drawing up a will. I hope it will help you plan your affairs so you can pay less – perhaps a great deal less – tax. Whatever your course of action, you should consider taking professional advice as there are many pitfalls for the unwary.

The information in this book is based on the law and Inland Revenue practice as at 30 November 2003. You should watch out for subsequent changes made in the Pre-Budget Report of December 2003 and the Spring 2004 Budget.

2

Getting to grips with the basics

'WHY SHOULD I CARE about inheritance tax?' or 'Why should I worry about making a will?' are questions I often hear.

Whether or not you worry about inheritance tax (IHT) is really your personal choice. At the end of the day, IHT is not actually suffered by you and doesn't affect your lifestyle. Instead, it restricts the amount you leave behind for your family (your 'estate', defined in the box opposite).

Having said that, IHT is an expensive tax. There is a tax-free threshold (known as the 'nil-rate band', currently £255,000), but the rest of your estate is subject to tax at 40%, although there are various exemptions. You cannot get round this by giving everything away just before you die, because gifts in the seven years before death count as part of your estate for IHT purposes.

Note that the nil-rate band of £255,000 and the rate of 40% are current for the tax year 2003/04, but these are subject to annual change in the Spring Budget.

The table on page 8 shows the tax due on various sizes of estate and the effective tax rate. As you can see, an estate of £500,000 could lose almost one-fifth of its value in tax. But it is not all doom and gloom. If the thought of a large part of

Calculating your 'estate'

Your estate is basically the total of all your assets less your liabilities, such as your mortgage and credit card balances.

What should you include in the calculation of your estate?

Family home

Household contents

Personal effects, i.e. jewellery etc.

Bank and building society accounts

Shares and securities

National Savings investments

Pension fund lump sums

PEPS/ISAs

Life assurance

Holiday homes

Cars/boats

Money owed to you

Other assets

Your share of jointly owned assets

What can you deduct from the calculation of your estate?

Mortgage

Credit card debt

Car loans

Other money owed by you

your estate going to the taxman depresses you, do not despair. There are lots of reliefs and exemptions that are available – for example, gifts to a spouse are tax-free – and with careful planning the taxman's share of the cake can be substantially reduced.

When embarking on an IHT planning exercise, the first step is to consider your current capital position, and how

Tax due on estate

Value of estate, £	Tax due, £	Effective tax rate, %
250,000	–	0
500,000	98,000	19.6
750,000	198,000	26.4
1,000,000	298,000	29.8
2,000,000	698,000	34.9
3,000,000	1,098,000	36.6

much tax there might be on your estate. The next step is to write a will (see page 10), to ensure that you make the most of your nil-rate band and any other reliefs and exemptions that are available. Once you have done this, you might want to consider giving money away during your lifetime. Lifetime gifts are generally tax-free if they are made more than seven years before your death. This is covered in Chapter 3. However, before you consider lifetime giving you need to look at your current income and financial needs to decide what you can afford to give.

The first step

Working out your current capital position involves a valuation of all your assets and liabilities. The table opposite gives you an example of a capital statement.

How much tax?

Once you have your capital statement, you will be able to

Example: drawing up a capital statement

Mr and Mrs Badger have the following assets:

Assets and liabilities at current values

Assets	Mr Badger £	Mrs Badger £
Family home	375,000	–
Household contents and personal effects	22,000	–
Bank and building society accounts	45,000	16,000
Shares and securities	22,000	20,000
National Savings investments	–	–
Pension fund lump sums	80,000	–
Other financial assets e.g. PEPs/ISAs	12,000	–
Life assurance	120,000	–
Holiday home	180,000	–
Car	25,000	–
Other assets	8,000	–
Money owed to them	–	–
TOTAL ASSETS	889,000	36,000
Liabilities		
Mortgage (covered by separate life insurance cover)	180,000	–
Bank loans and/or overdraft	5,000	1,000
Credit cards	5,000	1,000
Hire purchase agreements	–	–
Other liabilities e.g. funeral expenses	3,500	3,500
TOTAL LIABILITIES	(193,500)	(5,500)
VALUE OF ESTATE	£695,500	£30,500

work out your likely IHT liability based on the current value of your estate. As you can see from the example of Mr and Mrs Badger, your financial position may change on death; for example your mortgage may be repaid on your death if you have life insurance for it. Not everybody does and this depends on the type of mortgage you have taken out, so check with your bank or building society. Your life insurance policy may also be 'written into trust' so that the proceeds don't fall into your estate for IHT purposes – see Chapter 5 for more on insurance.

You also need to take into account the way in which your estate is distributed on death. For example, gifts to your spouse are tax-free, so if you leave all your assets to your husband or wife there will be no IHT liability on your death. However, if you do this, you are wasting your valuable nil-rate band (as your estate is already tax-free). The example opposite, calculating Mr and Mrs Badger's IHT liability, illustrates the position.

Writing a will

The most important aspect of IHT planning is writing a will. According to research carried out for the Halifax more than half of us don't prepare a will, even though most of us see the need for one. So why is having a will so important?

Well, without a will the assets you leave behind may not get left to the people you really want to have them, and the professional costs of winding up your estate are more expensive. If you should die without a will, you die what is known as 'intestate' and there are special rules that govern who will receive your assets. These rules are set out in the table on pages 12 and 13.

If you die intestate, the IHT liability on your estate could

Example: estimated IHT position for Mr and Mrs Badger

Mr and Mrs Badger from the previous example have not undertaken any IHT planning. They have basic wills that leave all assets to the surviving spouse.

Mr Badger dies first and leaves all his assets to Mrs Badger. As the mortgage is covered by life insurance, he leaves Mrs Badger with assets of £889,000 minus debts of £13,500 – £875,500 in total. There is no IHT due at this stage because Mr Badger has left everything to his wife.

On Mrs Badger's death, the IHT due will be as follows:

	£
Estate from Mr Badger	875,500
Mrs Badger's net assets	30,500
Total net assets	906,000
Less: nil-rate band	(255,000)
Taxable estate	651,000
IHT at 40%	£260,400

Although Mr Badger's estate was tax-free, it has pushed Mrs Badger into the IHT bracket, and his nil-rate band has been wasted. With some simple planning, Mrs Badger's IHT liability could have been reduced. For example, adding a clause to Mr Badger's will to set up a discretionary will trust, as described in the example of Mr and Mrs Fox on page 15, could have saved an additional £102,000.

be more than it should otherwise be, because the intestacy rules may not make the best use of all the exemptions and reliefs available. A will also enables you to leave instructions, for example about your burial, and gives you the opportunity to nominate the persons you would like to look after and

Intestacy rules

The rules differ depending whether or not you die with 'issue'. Your 'issue' are your children and, if they pre-decease you, their children and so on. If children inherit before the age of 18, their inheritance must be kept in a 'statutory trust' on their behalf until they reach that age, or earlier in some circumstances (usually marriage). Until then, the trust works rather like an accumulation and maintenance trust, as discussed in Chapter 9.

Spouse and issue survive
Spouse receives
£125,000 outright
All personal chattels (i.e. belongings but not cash)
Life interest in one half of the residue (i.e. a right to income)

Issue receive
One half of residue plus the other half of residue upon death of spouse

Spouse survives without issue
Spouse receives
£200,000 outright
All personal chattels
One half of residue outright

Remainder shared between
The deceased's parents

If no parent survives:
the deceased's brothers and sisters (but not half-brothers and half-sisters) and their issue

Spouse survives but no issue, parents, brothers or sisters or their issue
Whole estate to surviving spouse

No spouse survives
Estate held for the following in the order given. Please note that you will only benefit if there is nobody in the previous category, or they have all pre-deceased you. For example, your parents will only benefit if you have no issue.

a) Issue of the deceased
b) Parents
c) Brothers and sisters and their issue
d) Half-brothers and half-sisters and their issue
e) Grandparents
f) Uncles and aunts and their issue
g) Half-brothers and half-sisters of the deceased's parents and their issue
h) The Crown, the Duchy of Lancaster or the Duchy of Cornwall

Note that these rules apply to England and Wales – different rules apply in Scotland and Northern Ireland.

distribute your estate. You can also say who you would like to be the legal guardians of your children, should the need arise.

The following example shows how dying intestate can mean a larger IHT bill than necessary, because valuable reliefs and exemptions may not be used.

Example: IHT if you die intestate

Mr Hamster dies intestate. He has an estate of £800,000, which includes personal belongings of £15,000. He leaves behind a wife and two young children.

Mrs Hamster will receive the following assets:

	£
Personal chattels	15,000
£125,000 absolutely	125,000
Life interest in 50% of the balance	330,000
Total	£ 470,000

The balance of £330,000 is left on trust for the children. Gifts to a spouse are tax-free so there is no IHT on Mrs Hamster's share of the estate. However, there will be an IHT bill on the children's share as follows:

	£
Taxable estate	330,000
Less: nil-rate band	(255,000)
Taxable estate	£75,000
IHT at 40%	£30,000

If Mr Hamster had made a will leaving more of his estate to his wife, the £30,000 IHT could have been saved.

It is even more important for co-habitees and same-sex couples that a will is made. Your estate could pass to your parents or other relatives rather than to your long-term partner. All is not lost if you die intestate, as there is an opportunity for the position to be altered within two years of your death through a 'deed of variation' (covered in Chapter 4). However, the situation is likely to be more expensive and upsetting for everyone.

Although dying intestate can be expensive, if you write a will that leaves all your assets directly to your spouse, you are wasting your valuable nil-rate band. You can avoid this by leaving assets to your children, rather than your husband or wife, but this may not be practical if most of your estate is made up of the value of your home. Instead, you could include a provision in your will for the creation of a 'Discretionary

---

Example: A simple way to save £102,000

Mrs and Mrs Fox have a joint estate worth £510,000, which they own in equal shares. On Mr Fox's death, if he leaves all his assets (£255,000) to his wife, there is no IHT liability. However, on Mrs Fox's death there is an IHT liability of £102,000. If Mr Fox had left his assets in a discretionary will trust of which Mrs Fox and their children are beneficiaries, he would still have no IHT liability, as his gift to the trust would be below the nil-rate band. The trustees could make discretionary income payments to Mrs Fox. On Mrs Fox's death, her IHT liability would also be nil as her estate is below the nil-rate band. A simple way to save £102,000!

Will Trust' equal to the nil-rate band. This is a discretionary trust that is set up by adding a special clause to your will. The trustees have the discretion to pay income and/or capital to a list of named beneficiaries. Trusts are dealt with in further detail in Chapter 9.

The advantage of a discretionary will trust is that your wife could be a beneficiary of the trust and receive income from it. Your gift to the trust is tax-free because it falls within the nil-rate band, but the taxable value of your estate is reduced by the same amount.

Working out your surplus income

Having reviewed the likely IHT and dealt with your will, you might want to consider reducing the tax bill for your family by giving money away during your lifetime. Before you do this, it is necessary to look at your current income position and financial needs, then decide what you can afford to give away.

As part of this it is necessary to consider your likely items of annual expenditure. Some of these are set out in the table opposite.

The final step before embarking on any serious IHT planning is to consider your future income requirements. As the example of Mr and Mrs Badger on page 18 shows, you have to ensure that there is sufficient wealth to meet future living expenditure, and you must also build in a buffer for the unexpected, for example to meet medical and nursing bills.

Armed with all this information you can now establish

Checklist of outgoings

These are your likely items of annual expenditure

- Mortgage interest
- Council tax
- Water rates
- Rent
- Gas
- Electricity
- Telephone bill
- House repairs and improvement
- Insurance – home, car, health
- Loan interest
- Maintenance payments
- Holidays
- Subscriptions (golf club etc.)
- Charitable donations
- Clothes
- Car expenses
- Medical bills
- School fees/childcare
- Food bills
- Spending money, entertainment etc.
- Gifts
- Tax

how much you wish to give away to family and friends during your lifetime.

Example: working out surplus income

Let's continue with the example of Mr and Mrs Badger. The example on page 9 shows their capital position. They work out their surplus income for 2003/04 as follows:

	Mr Badger, £	Mrs Badger, £
Taxable income	195,000	5,000
Tax	(72,000)	(500)
Net spendable income	123,000	4,500
Less: estimated annual expenditure	(82,000)	(1,000)
Surplus income	£41,000	£3,500

This shows that Mr Badger has plenty of surplus income at the moment, but before he gives it all away he needs to think about what will be his future position. How will his income change, for example on retirement? And what will Mrs Badger's position be if he pre-deceases her?

3

Lifetime giving

As MENTIONED IN Chapter 1, IHT has often been called a voluntary tax. This is because with careful planning, by using the various exemptions, IHT on death can be minimised. The most important and valuable relief is that most gifts made more than seven years before death are exempt from IHT. It is therefore essential to plan early. This is known as the 'seven-year rule' and is discussed further on page 21.

There are also specific exemptions for certain lifetime gifts, for example between husband and wife. These are covered on page 22.

If you decide to make lifetime gifts, there are a number of potential traps:

- It is not possible to have your cake and eat it. If you give something away, but continue to benefit from it, you may be caught by the gift with reservation of benefit provisions – for example if you give your children your house and continue to live there, it will remain within your estate for IHT purposes. These rules are covered on page 28.
- Your gift may be liable for capital gains tax (see page 26).

■ You need to be clear whether the recipient, or your estate, will pay any tax on death (see page 30).

The practical considerations

The best advice in many situations is simply to enjoy your lifestyle, and spend as much as you want. If there is some left for your relatives at the end of it, then good for them!

The most sophisticated IHT planning is no use to you at all if you have given your capital away and do not have sufficient resources to live on in your old age.

Family relationships must also be considered. Relationships with your children may be good now, but what about in ten years' time? Remember what happened to King Lear.

Think about the consequences of your children getting married or divorced. And think carefully about giving directly to your children at an early age, as they may squander the money or become less independent. This is when trusts may be useful. See Chapter 9 for more information on trusts.

Asset selection

When passing assets to your family, you should examine your capital statement and surplus income (covered in Chapter 2), and decide which assets to gift. If you need to maintain your existing income levels, then consider gifting non-income-producing assets, such as paintings or cars.

While rapidly appreciating assets are good investments, they aggravate the IHT problem by swelling the value of your estate. So, it might be advisable to gift these as early as possible.

Generation skipping

When making gifts, you should also consider the IHT position of the recipient. Your children, for example, may be financially secure and you could just be lumbering them with an additional IHT liability. It may be better to make gifts directly to your grandchildren or, if they are young, to a trust set up for their benefit.

The seven-year rule

The seven-year rule applies to most lifetime gifts. It means that the following gifts are tax-free so long as they are made more than seven years before your death:

- Gifts to individuals
- Gifts into an accumulation and maintenance trust
- Gifts into an interest in possession trust
- Gifts into a trust for the disabled

Trusts are explained in further detail in Chapter 9.

The gifts listed above are known as potentially exempt transfers (PETs) and can give valuable IHT savings, as illustrated in the table on page 22.

Another advantage of making PETs is that although they count as part of your estate, if you die within seven years of making them but survive for at least three years, a special 'taper relief' will apply. This is covered in Chapter 4.

Potential IHT savings on lifetime transfers

Value of estate before gift	Potential reduction in IHT on PETs made more than seven years before death			
£	Gift £50,000	£100,000	£150,000	£200,000
300,000	18,000	18,000	18,000	18,000
350,000	20,000	38,000	38,000	38,000
400,000	20,000	40,000	58,000	58,000
500,000	20,000	40,000	60,000	80,000
1,000,000	20,000	40,000	60,000	80,000

Chargeable lifetime transfers

Note that gifts into a discretionary trust are not classed as PETs. Instead, they are called chargeable lifetime transfers and there will be an immediate tax bill if they, plus any chargeable transfers in the previous seven years, exceed the nil-rate band. Any tax payable is charged at a maximum of 20% (the lifetime rate, which is half the rate on death) but more tax may be payable at a later stage – see Chapter 4.

Lifetime exemptions

The following lifetime gifts are tax-free altogether.

Husband and wife

Transfers between husband and wife are exempt from IHT during their lifetimes or on death. But if your husband or wife is not 'UK domiciled' (explained in Chapter 10), then only the first £55,000 of the transfer is exempt.

For this exemption to apply you must be legally married and not just living together as husband and wife in a common law marriage. Reform is due in this area as there are more and more co-habitee arrangements and gay 'marriages'. The Civil Partnership Bill announced in the 2003 Queen's Speech sets out to extend rights given to married couples to people in a legally recognised 'civil partnerships' scheme, but only in England and Wales. The tax position is likely to be addressed in the future.

As lifetime gifts between individuals are exempt if they are made more than seven years before death, the ages of the husband and wife should be taken into account when deciding who should make the gift to the intended recipient. If possible, the spouse who is most likely to survive seven years should make the gift.

Annual exemption

You are entitled to an annual exemption of £3,000. This means that you can make gifts totalling up to £3,000 tax-free in any one tax year. If you do not use the exemption in one year, it can be carried forward to the next year, but no further. The examples on pages 24 and 61 show how this works.

Small gifts exemption

Gifts of £250 or less to any one individual are tax-free, but this doesn't apply if the total gifts made to that individual in one tax year exceed £250 (so it cannot be combined with the annual exemption). There is no limit to the number of small gifts that you can make to different individuals.

Example: carrying forward the annual exemption

Mrs Ewe makes a gift of £5,000 to her cousin during the tax year 2003/04. She did not make any gifts during 2002/03. Her position is therefore as follows:

		£
2002/03	No gifts made – exemption carried forward	3,000
2003/04	Gifts of £5,000 made	5,000
	Annual exemption for 2003/04	(3,000)
	Brought forward from 2002/03	(2,000)

The whole of Mrs Ewe's gift is tax-free, but £1,000 of her 2002/03 exempt amount is unused and its benefit is lost.

Regular gifts out of surplus income

If your income is more than sufficient to meet your annual spending needs, regular gifts out of your surplus income are tax-free. You should be able to work out how much you can comfortably give away by calculating your net spendable income and setting this against your likely outgoings. In the case of Mr and Mrs Badger on page 18, they have surplus income of over £44,000 that they could consider gifting in this way.

It is helpful to have some documentation in place at the time the gifts are made in order to show that they are made out of surplus income. You do not, however, need Revenue agreement before you make the payments; this will normally be dealt with after your death, when the personal representatives are agreeing the IHT position.

Gifts on marriage

You can give the following amounts free of IHT to somebody who is getting married:

- Up to £5,000 from each parent
- Up to £2,500 from each grandparent
- Up to £1,000 from any other person

Gifts to charity

Gifts to charity are exempt not only from IHT, but usually also from income tax and capital gains tax.

Other exemptions

- In most cases gifts for the support and maintenance of children and dependent relatives
- Gifts to a qualifying political party
- A gift for a national purpose (such as a gift to the National Gallery or the British Museum)
- A gift for the public benefit (such as a gift of an historic building to a non-profit-making trust)
- A gift of heritage property or work of art, and so on, even if it remains in private ownership, provided that the public is given reasonable access to it and it is kept in good order
- Maintenance funds for historic buildings

There are certain conditions to be met for some of the above exemptions to apply. It is unlikely that some of these will apply other than in the most extraordinary circumstances. If you have a stately pile then you unquestionably need – but probably already get – specialist help.

Capital gains tax implications

Capital gains tax must also be considered. When you give something away you are treated for tax purposes as if you have sold it, and capital gains tax – a tax on profits made when you dispose of a capital asset – may therefore apply. Broadly speaking, you pay tax on the current market value of the asset, minus its value when you acquired it (its 'base cost'), subject to various reliefs and exemptions.

The tax is payable at the same rate as the income tax you pay on your savings income – i.e. at 10 per cent if you are a starting-rate taxpayer, at 20 per cent if you are a basic-rate taxpayer, or 40 per cent if you are a higher-rate taxpayer. However, tax is only payable if your total taxable capital gains in any one tax year come to more than the annual exemption (£7,900 in 2003/04).

Transfers between husband and wife are tax-free provided the spouses are living together during the relevant tax year. Care must be taken in the tax year following separation as a capital gains tax charge could arise on disposals of assets between estranged spouses. Certain assets are free of capital

---

Example: capital gains tax on a gift

Mr Squirrel gives a painting worth £50,000 to his son in October 2003. He bought the painting two years earlier at a car boot sale for £50. For capital gains tax purposes, there is a taxable gain of £49,950 arising on the gift. Assuming that Mr Squirrel has already used his annual exemption and is a higher-rate taxpayer, he will have to pay capital gains tax on the gift of £49,950 x 40% = £19,980.

gains tax in any event; for example, cash, motor cars and some yachts.

In some instances, the capital gains tax liability can be deferred by making a 'holdover' election. The effect of making such an election is that the recipient takes over your base cost for capital gains tax purposes, assuming that no cash passes hands. Holdover relief can only be claimed on:

- A gift of 'business assets' by an individual to another individual or trust. Business assets include shares in an unlisted trading company, shares in a quoted company if you own more than 5%, or business assets used for a trade carried on by any such company, or by you as a sole trader.
- A gift of any assets to a discretionary trust.

So, in the example opposite, Mr Squirrel would not be able to claim holdover relief on the gift to his son, but the following example shows a situation in which holdover relief could be claimed.

Example: holdover relief

Mr Rabbit gives his son his Crazy Carrots Ltd shareholding, which counts as a business asset. The shares' current market value is £150,000 and their original base cost was £50,000, giving rise to a £100,000 capital gain. Holdover relief is claimed, so no capital gains is payable at the time, but when Mr Rabbit Junior eventually parts with the shares, his base cost is also £50,000.

There is no capital gains tax on death, and the beneficiaries of your estate will inherit your assets at the market value at the date of your death. For example, if your house cost £100,000 in 1994 and it is worth £250,000 on your death, your beneficiaries will receive it at a value of £250,000. This will also be their base cost for capital gains tax purposes. Therefore, if they sell the property six months after your death for £260,000, they will only pay capital gains tax on £10,000.

As this shows, you need to weigh up the potential IHT and capital gains tax savings when deciding which assets to give. It can be a careful balancing act.

Gifts with reservation of benefit

You may be happy to give your home to your children so long as you may continue to live there for the rest of your life. You may quite like to give your children some cash, but continue to receive the income from it or reserve the right to call the money back if you should need it later in life.

Having your cake and eating it in this way would be ineffective for IHT. A gift is only exempt if it is made outright and with 'no strings attached'. The rules covering what are known as 'gifts with reservation of benefit' are complex and unfortunately it is not possible to go along to the Inland Revenue and ask if they apply in any given situation.

If a gift is caught by these rules, then the asset is still deemed to be yours for IHT purposes. It only becomes effective for IHT when you cease to draw any benefit from it. These rules are particularly harsh. As the judge put it in one tax case, 'not only may you not have your cake and eat it, but if you eat more than a few crumbs of what was given, you are deemed for tax purposes to have eaten the lot!'

The Inland Revenue has given guidance on the benefits you may receive in respect of property gifted without bringing these rules into play, for example the following would be permitted:

- You give your house to your son and your son lives in it. You may stay there for up to two weeks a year.
- You give a car to your daughter and she gives you occasional lifts in that car (i.e. less than three times a month).

On the other hand, the following are examples of benefits to which the Inland Revenue consider that the gift with reservation rules would apply:

- You give your house to your son and then stay there most weekends.
- You give your daughter a car and she gives you a lift to work every day.

There are two situations where you may give something away and still benefit from it without the 'reservation of benefit' rules applying:

- If you pay a full market rent for the use of the land or asset. So, if you give your house to your children but continue to live there, the property will remain in your estate for IHT purposes. However, if you pay your children a full market rent for continuing to live there then the property will no longer form part of the estate. It may be easy to calculate a market rent for a property, but not so easy for paintings, say, you have gifted that continue to hang in the house.

■ If you give property to a relative (for example your children), or to your husband's or wife's relative, but then you are forced by age or infirmity, say, to move back in. However, this would only apply if the change in your circumstances was unforeseen when the gift was made, and it represents a reasonable provision for your care and maintenance. This would also apply if, for example, you gave away cash that was subsequently needed for healthcare.

The second exception is unlikely to be of useful practical assistance, although in some circumstances the first exception might be.

Who pays the tax?

Finally, when you make a gift, it needs to be made clear who should pay any IHT, if you do not survive for at least seven years. It could be your intention that any tax liability will be paid out of your estate or you may wish any tax charge to be met by the person receiving the gift. If you do not make your intentions known, then the estate will pay the tax. If the estate has insufficient funds, the Inland Revenue will then approach the recipient.

Note that the value of the gift for tax purposes will be the total loss to the estate. If you do not wish the recipient to pay

> ### Example: if the estate pays the tax
>
> Mr Sheep gives £120,000 to his son Lamb. His previous gifts have already used up his nil-rate band. In the event of Mr Sheep's death, he would like the estate to pay any IHT on the gift. He dies within two years of the gift so no taper relief is due. In order to calculate the amount on which tax is payable, the gift is grossed up by two-thirds, as follows:
>
> | | £ |
> |---|---:|
> | Gift made by Mr Sheep | 120,000 |
> | Add ⅔ of £120,000 | 80,000 |
> | Gift subject to IHT (loss to the estate) | 200,000 |
> | IHT at 40% payable by the estate | £ 80,000 |
>
> If Mr Sheep had wanted Lamb to pay the tax, the loss to Mr Sheep's estate would be only £120,000. The tax at 40% would be £48,000 and the overall benefit of the gift for Lamb would be £72,000 (£120,000 - £48,000).

any tax on the gift, and the tax is met from your estate, the taxable amount is the value of the gift itself plus the IHT payable. However, the tax works out at two-thirds of the gift (not 40%), because it is calculated on the loss to the estate (the figures are slightly different if the gift qualifies for taper relief, see page 37). See above for the 'Mr Sheep' example of 'grossing-up', as this calculation is called.

If the recipient is to pay the tax, then the loss to the estate is just the amount of the gift. However, you can take out life insurance that would provide the recipient with enough cash to pay any tax on your death. For more on suitable life insurance see Chapter 5.

4

On death

IF YOU HAVE A WILL, you have probably nominated executors to deal with your estate on your death. Otherwise, your estate will pass in accordance with the rules on intestacy (see Chapter 2) and your heirs will be appointed to act as administrators. Your executors or administrators are called 'personal representatives' and are responsible for:

- valuing your estate and working out the tax on it (see below)
- claiming any appropriate reliefs or exemptions (see page 36)
- paying any IHT due. Payment is due within six months of your death. This can give rise to difficulties for some personal representatives, for example where the main asset of the estate is the family home. But see page 39 for various ways of funding the tax.

Valuing your estate

The personal representatives dealing with your estate will need to make the fullest possible enquiries into your affairs in order to ascertain its value. By going through the papers and making enquiries on what may be the slimmest of leads they will piece together a picture of the estate. If you are acting as a personal representative then the Inland Revenue's Probate and IHT Helpline can explain how to apply for probate, and will supply forms and advise on their completion. Further information can be found on the Inland Revenue website (www.inlandrevenue.gov.uk).

The personal representatives will submit form IHT 200 to Inland Revenue Capital Taxes to give details of the assets and liabilities at the date of death (your estate). They can deal with the papers themselves, or they can instruct a solicitor to do so on their behalf.

Schedules attached to form IHT 200 will provide details of assets that you gave away in the seven years prior to death. These are included at their market value at the date of the gift, but if their value has fallen since then, the market value at the date of death can be used instead. (If the value of the asset has increased no adjustment is required.) Gifts of assets from which you still benefit ('gifts with reservation of benefit') must be included. As explained in Chapter 3, these remain part of your estate for IHT purposes.

You may also have had an 'interest in possession' in trust funds (see Chapter 9). The trust funds in which you have an interest count as part of your estate for calculating your IHT liability. The trustees will return details of the interest in the trust fund using form IHT 100.

All of the values that are returned on these forms are added together to give your chargeable estate on death. Deductions are made for any reliefs and the nil-rate band (using the figure that applies in the tax year of death – £255,000 for deaths in the 2003/04 tax year). The rest of your estate, after deductions, is charged to IHT at the rate of 40%.

Excepted estates

If you die leaving an estate of £240,000 or less, you need to complete another less detailed form instead of form IHT 200. The limit of £240,000 applies for deaths occurring after 5 April 2003 and is subject to change from time to time.

There are restrictions to the use of the excepted estates arrangements. For example, these arrangements are not available if more than £100,000 of your estate is represented by trust property or if property of more than £75,000 is situated outside the UK. Additionally, they will not apply if you have made gifts of more than £100,000 in the seven years before your death.

Who pays the tax?

The recipient of a lifetime gift is liable to pay any tax due on the gift on your death, unless you have made arrangements for the tax to be met out of the estate (see page 31). The same applies if you have transferred money to a trust – the trustees are liable. Your personal representatives are liable to pay any other tax. If more than one person is liable to pay the tax due, the overall tax charge is split between them in line with the proportion of the estate to which they are entitled. This is demonstrated in the example opposite.

Example: how much tax?

Mr Monkey died in August 2003, leaving an estate of £750,000. He had a life interest in a trust fund of £250,000. He had also made PETs of £255,000 within the previous seven years. The total tax due is £400,000.

	Chargeable amount, £	Tax, £
PETs made within seven years of death	255,000	
Less: nil-rate band available	(255,000)	
	Nil	Nil
Estate on death	750,000	
Trust fund in which Mr Monkey had a life interest	250,000	
	£1,000,000	
	@ 40% =	400,000

The IHT due is apportioned as follows between the estate and the trustees.

Tax on estate

$£400,000 \times \dfrac{£750,000}{£1,000,000} = £300,000$

Payable by personal representatives

Tax on trust fund

$£400,000 \times \dfrac{£250,000}{£1,000,000} = £100,000$

Payable by trustees

Chargeable lifetime transfers

It was mentioned in Chapter 3 that tax may be payable during your lifetime on gifts into a discretionary trust, at the lifetime rate of 20%, if you have already used up the nil-rate band. Any such gifts that were made within seven years of death become part of the net chargeable estate on which tax at 40% will be paid. An allowance is made for the tax paid previously at the lifetime rates.

Warning: exempt and non-exempt legacies

Where the balance of your estate, after specific legacies have been made, is left to some beneficiaries who enjoy exempt status (i.e. your spouse and charities) and others who are not exempt, it is advisable to say in your will how the IHT is to be allocated. In the absence of specific directions making it clear that the tax burden is not to fall on the exempt beneficiaries, they will be left paying part of the tax.

Exemptions and reliefs

Surviving spouse
In the same way that lifetime gifts between husband and wife are exempt (see page 22), gifts to the surviving spouse are exempt on death. This can be the gift of assets from the estate or may apply where your life interest in a trust fund has come to an end and there is a further interest in favour of your surviving spouse.

For this exemption to apply you must be legally married and not just living together as husband and wife in a common law marriage.

Taper relief

If you made gifts within the seven years prior to your death they will become chargeable to IHT on your death. If the total of the gifts is within the nil-rate band then there will be no tax to pay on those gifts, but if a liability does arise the tax payable on gifts made between three and seven years of death will be reduced as follows:

Period between gift and death	Rate of reduction in tax liability
3–4 years	20%
4–5 years	40%
5–6 years	60%
6–7 years	80%

Example: taper relief on gifts within seven years of death

Mrs Bear gives assets worth £300,000 to her son, having made no previous gifts. They are worth £350,000 when she dies four and a half years later.

	Chargeable amount, £	Tax, £
Chargeable gift	300,000	
Less nil-rate band	255,000	
	45,000	@ 40% = 18,000
Less: taper relief of 40%		(7,200)
IHT payable		£10,800

Note that the gift is pooled with all the other assets of your estate and does not attract an additional nil-rate band. As the gift has used up all of Mrs Bear's nil-rate band, the whole of her estate at death will be subject to IHT at 40%.

Succession relief

Relief is given for those situations where someone dies within five years of inheriting assets on which IHT has been paid. To avoid a second burden of tax on the same assets, a proportion of the IHT paid on the first death will be deducted from the tax charge due on the second death.

The proportion of the tax relieved is as follows:

Period between deaths	*Relief*
Less than 1 year	100%
1–2 years	80%
2–3 years	60%
3–4 years	40%
4–5 years	20%

Example: succession relief

Mr Gerbil has a chargeable estate of £500,000. On his death, his estate includes a painting worth £150,000, which was valued at £100,000 two and a half years earlier when it was left to him by his father. On his father's death IHT of £40,000 was paid on the painting.

	£
IHT on Mr Gerbil's estate of £500,000	98,000
Less: Relief for tax paid on painting by father's estate (60% of £40,000)	(24,000)
Total IHT payable by Mr Gerbil's estate	£74,000

Assets that fall in value

Relief may be claimed for some assets sold within a short period of your death, at a value that is lower than the probate value. This applies to certain qualifying investments (such as quoted shares) sold within a year of your death, or to land or property sold within three years of your death. In these cases the sale proceeds may be taken as the basis for working out the IHT, instead of the probate value. The claim must relate to all of the qualifying investments sold, not just those sold at a loss.

Other exemptions and reliefs

The following exemptions and reliefs, covered elsewhere in this book, are also available on death:

- Charitable bequests – see page 25
- Business property relief – see page 57
- Agricultural property relief – see page 67
- Woodlands – see page 67
- Assets of national importance – see page 68

Funding the IHT

When the application is made for the grant of probate, the personal representatives have to make an initial payment of IHT. This initial payment does not include the liability on any freehold property or on any assets for which they are claiming to pay by instalments.

The personal representatives may have to organise a loan for the payment of this liability or they may be able to use cash from your bank and building society accounts. A new Inland Revenue scheme enables funds to be transferred electronically from banks and building societies in part settlement of the IHT liability.

Paying by instalments

Your personal representatives can elect to pay the IHT over a period of ten years by ten equal annual instalments. Interest is payable on the outstanding amount. This option only applies to certain assets as follows:

- Land (including the family home);
- Shares of a company in which you had control;
- Unquoted shares if payment of tax would give rise to hardship;
- A business, interest in a business, or unquoted shares worth at least £20,000 if their nominal value represents more than 10% of the total nominal value;
- Unquoted shares held at your death, provided that at least 20% of the total tax payable relates to these shares or to other assets for which tax can be paid by instalments.

If IHT is payable on a gift you made in the seven years before your death, the asset you gave away must still be held by the recipient for the instalment method to be claimed. If the relevant property has been sold, the outstanding tax (and interest) is payable immediately.

Acceptance in lieu

The Inland Revenue can accept important heritage objects in lieu of IHT. They may accept works of art, manuscripts and historic documents. Further information can be found at www.resource.gov.uk/action.ail

Deeds of variation

Within two years of the date of your death, it is possible for your beneficiaries to execute a deed of variation to change the provisions in your will or the allocation of assets if you die intestate. For IHT the redistribution will be treated as having been made by you.

This procedure enables a person who does not wish to receive a legacy from your estate to give the funds to someone else, and the usual seven-year survival period does not apply.

Another important benefit of deeds of variation is to save tax. In cases where the whole of the estate goes to your surviving spouse, the benefit of the nil-rate band will have been lost. By executing a deed of variation your surviving spouse can redirect assets that will not be required for future needs and make use of the available nil-rate band. This can avoid having to make lifetime gifts later on and removes the need to survive for the seven-year period.

Professional advice should be taken before entering into a variation and consideration should be given to the income tax and capital gains tax implications of such an arrangement.

However, do not rely on deeds of variation as a substitute for writing a will. Governments have on various occasions considered their removal and you should not rely on them being around in the future.

5

The need for insurance

INSURANCE AND INSURANCE-BASED PRODUCTS can form a valuable part of your overall IHT planning.

Essentially, there are two methods of dealing with a potential IHT bill. The first is to maximise lifetime gifts and use the various reliefs and exemptions discussed elsewhere in this book. This is unlikely to mitigate your IHT liability completely. Your estate is still likely to include your family home and the funds required to meet your future living expenses. The second method uses life assurance as a means of providing funds for your beneficiaries so that they can pay the tax. A combination of both methods should be used to draw up an effective estate tax plan.

Before undertaking an estate planning exercise, you should consider whether your family will be adequately protected on the death or disability of the chief earner.

You need to ask yourself, 'If I die tomorrow, will my family be able to maintain our current standard of living?' If the answer is 'no', and if the family income will be dramatically reduced, then life assurance protection could be a solution.

Whole of life and term assurance

There are a number of types of life assurance, but the two most commonly used to provide funds to pay IHT are 'whole of life' and 'term' assurance.

A whole of life policy pays out at whatever moment you die, but term assurance only pays out if you die within a limited period, and is suitable for the younger person. For example, you may believe that in ten years' time you will have accumulated sufficient wealth for your family not to need to rely on life assurance. There is no surrender value to term insurance policies, but they are normally cheaper because at the end of a ten-year plan you will have paid money for no return. The policy can be written so that you can later convert it to a whole of life policy.

You will need to look carefully at your capital and annual surplus income before taking out any life assurance policy so as to ensure that you can fund the premiums for as long as necessary.

Writing policies in trust

It is usual to write these policies into trust. This means that on your death, the proceeds of the policy will pass to trustees who will exercise their discretion as to who should receive the proceeds. You normally provide a letter of wishes indicating who you would like to benefit. This is not a legally binding document, but the trustees will generally follow your wishes. The insurance company usually has standard documents for you to use.

There are two advantages of writing a policy in trust. The first is that the policy proceeds are paid out upon production of the death certificate and this avoids probate and an unnecessary delay. The second is that the proceeds are paid to your beneficiaries free of any IHT. You should therefore give serious consideration to leaving the proceeds to your children and grandchildren. If they are left to your spouse, although there is no immediate IHT bill, the proceeds will fall into your spouse's estate on death and your family will have lost the potential tax saving.

The annual premiums are treated as a gift for IHT purposes, but the premiums may qualify for exemption as a regular gift out of your surplus income (see page 24). Additionally, you may have available the annual exemption of £3,000 (see page 23). Otherwise, the premiums count as a lifetime gift and provided you survive seven years, they will become exempt.

Joint policies

For a husband and wife the policy can be written on a joint-life basis. A joint-life 'first death' policy will pay out when the first spouse dies, whereas a joint-life 'surviving spouse' policy will pay out only when both spouses have died. You will need to decide which option is best for you. Typically, any IHT does not arise until the second death, and because premiums are cheaper on this basis, most families select the joint-life (surviving spouse) option.

Some insurance companies also offer joint-life policies for co-habitees and same-sex couples, although these are usually more expensive than husband-and-wife policies. This is because there is no spouse exemption for non-married couples.

Covering a lifetime gift

Most lifetime gifts are 'Potentially Exempt Transfers' or 'PETs', covered in Chapter 3. The problem with a PET is that at the time of the gift, both you and the recipient are unsure whether it will escape IHT. It will only do so if you survive seven years from the date of the gift (although the tax due decreases over time because of taper relief; see page 37).

A special term assurance policy called a 'gift inter-vivos' assurance policy can provide a lump sum to pay the tax in the event of death within seven years. These life policies are structured on a seven-year 'decreasing term' basis. This means that the amount of insurance gradually decreases in line with the likely IHT liability, so that you are not paying for excess life assurance. In the event of death during the seven years the policy will pay out a lump sum to the recipient (via a trust) who can then pay the IHT.

As with other life assurance policies, the premiums paid will be treated as a gift for IHT purposes.

Pensions – death in service benefits

Private pension schemes, either company or personal, will usually provide for a payment to be made on your death. These 'death in service' benefits are usually written into trust and therefore fall outside your estate for IHT purposes. There is the opportunity to pay the benefits directly to your children or grandchildren. This will usually be dealt with by a letter of wishes or nomination form provided by the trustees or insurance company.

Key man insurance

If you are the driving force behind your family company or business, then its value could be significantly depleted if you die or suffer a critical illness. You should therefore consider a key man insurance policy. This would help the business by producing a capital sum on your death or critical illness, whilst confidence and profitability is restored in the company. The tax treatment differs depending upon the type of policy. Generally, however, the premiums are tax-deductible, whilst any proceeds are taxable.

Insurance-based products

There are also various insurance-based products that may assist in your overall estate planning exercise. These are generally provided by the large insurance companies and their suitability will depend upon your personal circumstances. The products will usually involve some form of trust and insurance bond and are typically known as, for example, 'discounted gift trust' and 'gift and loan' schemes.

There is generally a minimum contribution to these types of scheme. Your financial adviser will be able to offer you a variety, but remember that one size does not fit all. It is essential that you read the small print and take the advice of a tax adviser. The Chartered Institute of Taxation has a list of members that can be found via their website (at www.tax.org.uk).

Make sure you consider whether the product meets your overall requirements. For example, can you withdraw income or capital?

6

The family home

WITH THE MASSIVE INCREASE in property prices over the last few years, the family home is causing a real headache for many in terms of IHT. If, as shown in the example opposite, the remainder of your estate is not sufficient to cover the IHT liability, this can present your dependants with a real practical problem, because the tax is due just six months after your death. There is an option to pay by instalments (see Chapter 4), but in some cases, failure to plan carefully for the potential tax bill will mean that the family home has to be sold to pay the tax. This may not be what you and your family want.

According to Land Registry records, in August 2003 the average price of a detached house in Greater London was £515,720, with the average price of a terraced house at £255,104. Average prices of detached houses in the South East exceed the nil-rate band, currently £255,000, and they are only a few thousand pounds away in the South West.

Statistics show that five years ago, one in forty estates would have been subject to IHT because of the value of the family home. In five years' time, this will be one in eight.

The value of your family home, after deducting any mort-

Example: practical problems with property

Mr Horse, a widowed man, dies on 11 May 2003, leaving the following assets to his two children:

	£
House	450,000
Cash	55,000
	£505,000
IHT on: £255,000 (the nil-rate band)	Nil
£255,001 – £505,000 @ 40%	100,000
IHT due on 1 December 2003	£100,000

As you can see, there is pressure on the children to sell the house before 1 December in order to pay the liability. Otherwise they could consider paying the tax by instalments.

---

gage on the property, falls into your estate for IHT purposes. There are no general exemptions available. However, the sale of your main residence is not usually subject to capital gains tax. This is because there is a special 'main residence' exemption in respect of the family home. If you own more than one property, specialist advice should be obtained to ensure that the maximum capital gains tax relief can be claimed.

Simple planning

Inheritance tax planning around the family home has always been considered 'last resort planning'. Aside from the financial security a home offers, there are considerable emotional ties too.

For IHT purposes, you cannot simply give your house to your children and continue to live there rent-free. The complex rules concerning 'gifts with reservation of benefit' (covered on page 28) mean that the value of the house will remain within your estate. One way to get round this is to pay your children a full market rent and take on the risks of being a tenant at the mercy of your children!

Appropriate planning will depend upon your circumstances and a strategy that suits you may not suit your neighbour.

Term assurance

At a basic level, you may consider taking out term assurance to cover the potential IHT liability. This will be relatively cheap while you are young, and you could think about more complex planning later on in life. Insurance is covered in more detail in Chapter 5.

Mortgaging your property

Alternatively, with interest rates currently low, you may decide to take out a fixed rate mortgage on your property. The mortgage will reduce the value of the house for IHT purposes, but you then need to remove the cash proceeds of the mortgage from your estate. You could simply give your children the cash received from the mortgage and provided you survive seven years there will be no IHT to pay on the gift. You need to weigh up the cost of the mortgage interest against the likely tax saving.

Alternatively, you could use the cash to invest in assets that qualify for business property relief, for example, shares in your family trading company or unquoted shares. Business property relief is explained in further detail in Chapters 6 and 7. Provided you hold those shares for two years and all the other conditions are met, the relief will wipe out any liability to IHT on those assets. The commercial considerations of this route clearly need to be taken into account – you would be in a mess if you bought shares in companies that collapsed.

Sale of property to children

If your children have sufficient funds you could sell your house to them for its market value and then in due course, remove the cash from your estate, as outlined above. Your children could then allow you to live in the property rent-free, but you would, of course, be at the mercy of your children. Your children would generally have to pay stamp duty land tax. The capital gains tax implications must also be considered, as your children cannot claim the main residence exemption if they do not live there.

Tenants in common

Married couples usually own their home as joint tenants. This means that on your death, the house automatically passes to your spouse. As you are married, there is no IHT to pay on the first death. Although administratively this is the simplest route, it could be costing your family £102,000 in tax, because you are not making use of your nil-rate band. When

Example: joint ownership

Mr and Mrs Dalmatian live in a house worth £400,000 that they own in equal shares as tenants in common. They also have separate bank accounts each containing £50,000.

On Mrs Dalmatian's death, she leaves her share in the property and the cash to her children. Mr Dalmatian remains responsible for the general upkeep and maintenance of the property. On his death the remainder of his estate will be tax-free as it will be covered by his nil-rate band.

If Mr and Mrs Dalmatian had owned the property as joint tenants, Mrs Dalmatian's 50% share would have passed automatically to Mr Dalmatian on her death. There would have been no IHT liability at this point, as the transfer would have been covered by the spouse exemption. However, on Mr Dalmatian's death, the tax would have been:

	£
House	400,000
Cash	50,000
Estate	£450,000
IHT on £255,000 (the nil-rate band)	Nil
£255,001 – £450,000 @ 40%	78,000
IHT due	£78,000

As you can see, by simple planning, tax of £78,000 was saved. (Note that if the bank account had been in joint names, Mrs Dalmatian's half share would have also passed automatically to Mr Dalmatian.)

your spouse dies his or her estate will be increased by the value of the house. This is demonstrated in the examples on page 15 and above.

You could think about converting your joint tenancy so

that you own the property as tenants in common. This enables each of you to leave your share of the property to someone other than your husband or wife, thereby making use of your nil-rate band. However, there is always the problem with tenants in common that a joint owner could force a sale of the property.

If you are unsure whether you own your property as joint tenants or as tenants in common, your solicitor will be able to tell you. Note that different rules apply in Scotland (but not in Northern Ireland).

Unmarried couples

If you are an unmarried couple living together there is no IHT exemption available, even where you own the property as joint tenants. It is often preferable to own your property as tenants in common rather than joint tenants. This will enable your share to be passed on in accordance with your own wishes, even if there is no tax saving. For example, your will could provide for your share in the property to be transferred to your niece, but with your partner having the right to live there until his or her death. There are no particular IHT savings in this route, although it may be preferable from a family viewpoint. There are also risks with this strategy, as your partner might not feel comfortable with the idea of living in a property of which one half is owned by your niece.

As discussed in Chapter 3, in future the spouse exemption may be extended to unmarried couples living together, and this will be particularly beneficial in relation to the family home.

More complex planning

There are additional, more complex, arrangements available for IHT planning around the family home and the suitability of these depends upon your circumstances and your attitude towards tax planning and risk. These strategies may involve the use of a trust (or trusts) and possibly the creation of a lease or debt. The opinion of a barrister specialising in tax should generally be sought. Remember that it won't be you who will have to sort out these matters with the Inland Revenue and you may therefore wish to discuss your plans with those who will be inheriting the property.

The second property

Tax planning around the second property is more difficult. This is because there will be no main residence exemption available for capital gains tax purposes, and any lifetime gift may mean that you have to pay capital gains tax. Having said that, when buying the property a suitable structure for ownership should be considered.

For example, you may wish to put money into an accumulation and maintenance trust, which your grandchildren could use to acquire the property. Accumulation and maintenance trusts are explained in more detail in Chapter 9. The advantage is that the gift of cash to the trust counts as a 'potentially exempt' lifetime gift (a 'PET') and, provided you survive seven years, there is no IHT to pay. You should seek specialist advice in this area, particularly if you intend to stay at the second property from time to time, in case you are caught by the 'gifts with reservation of benefit' rules, as explained on page 28.

The overseas property

More and more of us are buying properties overseas. This can have many traps for the unwary. For example, France has rules stipulating who should receive certain property on your death, irrespective of what your will says. This means that your French 'chateau' may not necessarily pass in accordance with your wishes on your death. Many overseas jurisdictions have annual wealth taxes and gift taxes with which we are unfamiliar in the UK. Some countries will charge you to tax on the sale of the property, even if you are not resident there. It is essential when you are purchasing a property overseas to appoint a local lawyer with good English skills. You may require a local will that deals specifically with the property in that country.

Be cautious of acquiring a property overseas through a company. Traditionally, properties in Spain and Portugal were acquired through an 'offshore tax haven' company for local reasons. However, this can give rise to income tax problems in the UK if appropriate precautions are not taken. Owning the property via a trust may solve your problems, but again caution is the word, as many countries just do not understand what a trust is.

Generally speaking, in the case of property there will be some form of death duties to pay in the local jurisdiction, unless you are lucky enough to own a property in a country where there are no death duties, such as many of the

Caribbean Islands. If you are worried about your executors having to pay death duties in the other jurisdiction, do not despair. The Inland Revenue will usually allow such taxes to be offset against your UK IHT bill. You should seek specialist advice as this is a very complex area.

7

The family business

IF YOU OWN SHARES in a family company your IHT affairs need to be considered and planned carefully, as the value of your shares may form a large part of your estate.

The financial position of future generations may be dependent not only on the profitability and success of the company but also on careful IHT planning. Failure to plan could mean that some or all of the shares will have to be sold to pay the tax and the family would lose control of the business.

Business property relief

IHT on the shares in your family company can cause problems if the company is very profitable and the market value of the shares is very high. Business property relief is, therefore, a very important and valuable relief. There are two rates of relief: 100% and 50%.

Relief at 100% is available for the following assets:

- A business or interest in a business, i.e. sole trader or partnership;

- Any unquoted shares in a company; this includes shares listed on the Alternative Investment Market (AIM).

Relief at 50% is available for the following assets:

- Shares in a quoted company that you control;
- Any land or building, plant or machinery that is used wholly or mainly for the purposes of a business carried on by a company which you control or by a partnership of which you are a partner;
- Any land or building, plant or machinery used wholly or mainly for the purpose of a business you carry on, that is held by a trust of which you are a life tenant.

Business property relief is not available where the business consists wholly or mainly of:

- Dealing in securities, stock or shares;
- Dealing in land or buildings;
- The making or holding of investments.

These are called 'excepted assets'. An asset that is not used wholly or mainly for the purpose of the business concerned can also become an excepted asset, and relief is restricted in line with business use (see example opposite).

In order to qualify for relief on business property you must have owned the asset in question for at least two years. There are special rules for replacement assets.

It is therefore important to consider carefully whether all the conditions for relief are met, whether the company is a

> ## Example: business property relief
> Mr Lion makes a gift of an 80% unquoted shareholding in the family trading company to a discretionary trust, in January 2003. This qualifies for 100% business property relief.
> The company has been successful and the market value of the holding is £1.5m. At the date of the transfer the company owns assets worth £1.5m, of which £0.25m consists of the chairman's yacht. The yacht is an excepted asset for IHT purposes and so the relief is restricted in line with the proportion of excepted assets. Only $^{1.25}/_{1.5}$ of the full relief is available.
>
> Mr Lion's gift, for tax purposes, is:
>
> | | £ |
> |---|---|
> | Value of shares | 1,500,000 |
> | Less: business property relief | |
> | $^{1.25}/_{1.5}$ x 1,500,000 x 100% | 1,250,000 |
> | Gift for tax purposes | 250,000 |
>
> A gift to a discretionary trust is a chargeable lifetime transfer (see page 22) and so it is taxable immediately if it (plus previous taxable gifts) exceeds the nil-rate band. Clearly if Mr Lion's nil-rate band has already been used, the potential IHT charge is significant.

qualifying business for these purposes, and whether the value of any business property arises from 'excepted assets'.

Lifetime gifts

Shares in the family company are ideal assets to give away early. If the company is successful the shares are also likely to appreciate in value and are valuable assets in the hands of the recipients and this needs to be balanced with the fact that the base cost of the shares would be uplifted to market value on death (see page 28).

You need to consider the capital gains tax implications of giving away shares, but capital gains tax holdover relief (explained on page 26) may be available. You also need to think about whether your income is likely to be affected by a fall in your shareholding, if the company distributes profits to shareholders by way of dividends. You could instead draw profits by way of a salary to ensure that your level of income is maintained, but this may have adverse National Insurance implications.

Another practical problem may arise if you wish to ensure that you do not jeopardise your control over the company's major policy decisions. This position can be overcome by gifting your shares into a trust. If you are a trustee you can still control the voting rights of the shares.

A gift to a discretionary trust may be taxable immediately, if full business property relief is not available, but a gift to an interest in possession trust or accumulation and maintenance trust has no adverse IHT implications, provided you do not die within seven years of the transfer. These types of trust are explained further in Chapter 9. In this way, the shares can be passed for the benefit of your family without you losing voting control. It could also ensure that the shares do not need to be sold to pay IHT on death. Holdover relief for capital gains tax purposes (see page 26) may be available on the gift into the trust.

Another way of protecting against IHT on shares is to gift

Example: the business property relief trap

Mr Tiger gives an 80% unquoted shareholding in the family company valued at £500,000 to his son, Thomas, in November 1998. As Mr Tiger didn't use his £3,000 annual exemption in either that year or the following one (see page 23), £6,000 of the gift is immediately tax-free. The rest of the gift is taxable if Mr Tiger dies within 7 years, but it is potentially eligible for 100% business property relief. Thomas sells the shares in June 2000 and keeps the cash.

When Mr Tiger dies in October 2003 the gift becomes taxable and business property relief is denied as Thomas has sold the shares. However, it qualifies for taper relief at 40% because Mr Tiger survived for 4 years (see page 37). Mr Tiger's estate comprises of a house valued at £200,000 (which is tax-free because he left it to his wife) and other investments valued at £30,000, left to his son.

The IHT position on death is shown below.

Chargeable amount, £		Tax, £
PET now chargeable	494,000	
IHT on	255,000 (the nil-rate band)	Nil
	239,000 @ 40% =	95,600
Less taper relief @ 40%		(38,240)
Tax on gift of shares		57,360
Estate at death	30,000 @ 40% =	12,000
Total IHT due on death		£69,360

The family would be left with a tax liability of £69,360 on Mr Tiger's death and assets may need to be sold to pay this. If Thomas had retained the shares and qualified for business property relief no IHT would have been payable.

them to a charitable trust formed by the family. The value of the shares is taken outside the family as the shares are held for charitable purposes, but voting control is maintained.

A trap for lifetime transfers

As the example on page 61 shows, even if the conditions for granting business property relief are satisfied at the date of the original gift, failure to meet these conditions at death results in the denial of the relief.

A gift of business property should therefore be considered closely. For example, if you have given away shares that qualify for relief at the time of the gift and then die within seven years, the value of the gift is still included in the calculation of the IHT liability (although it may qualify for taper relief). The value of the gift will only be reduced by business property relief if the recipient still owns the shares (or has replaced them with other qualifying assets) and they still qualify for relief.

Therefore, if at the time of your death (within seven years of the gift) the recipient has sold the shares, there will be no business property relief available when calculating the IHT due.

Valuation

In the case of shares in an unquoted family company the problem is that there is no open market value for the shares. It is, therefore, necessary to undertake a share valuation.

There are many techniques for valuing shares but the

Example: valuing unquoted shares

Mr Hedgehog owns all the issued share capital in a company valued at £1m. He wishes to gift a 30% interest to a discretionary trust, leaving him with 70%. The agreed discounts which may normally be negotiated with the Inland Revenue might be as follows:

Shareholding, %	Discount, %
100	0
70	10
30	50

The value of the gift is as follows:

	£
Value of Mr Hedgehog's holding before gift:	
£1m @ 100%	1,000,000
Value of Mr Hedgehog's holding after gift:	
£1m @ 70% less 10% discount	630,000
Transfer for IHT purposes	£370,000
However, the value of the assets held by the discretionary trust is:	
£1m @ 30% less 50% discount	£150,000

important factor is that the value should reflect a hypothetical open market price that a willing buyer would pay a willing seller.

In calculating the taxable amount of a share transfer it is necessary to look at the value of your shareholding before and after the transfer. A discount will also need to be applied to shareholdings of less than 100% of the issued share capital of the company. This is because a 5% shareholding is worth less than 5% of the value of the company, as its voting rights have very little influence over the affairs of the company. Such valuations can sometimes provide surprising results, as the example above shows.

Buy and sell agreements

A final word of caution is due in respect of buy and sell agreements. It is common for partners or shareholder directors to agree that in the event of your death before retirement your personal representatives are obliged to sell and the survivors are obliged to purchase your shares. If you enter into such an agreement, then business property relief may be denied.

8

Tax-efficient investments

HAVING DETERMINED THE VALUE of your estate and the potential IHT, it is worth reviewing the assets comprised in your estate. You may not wish to give away any assets during your lifetime, but you could be interested in changing the mix of your estate to help reduce the tax you pay when you die.

By acquiring assets that give rise to IHT relief and disposing of assets that do not, the value of your estate may not change but your tax charge may fall. The assets that attract relief are set out in this chapter. Of course, you must keep in mind the capital gains tax consequences outlined on page 26, as well as considering the commercial implications, in order to ensure that the assets acquired will be suitable investments in other respects.

Some tax-efficient investments are described below, but if you are considering acquiring, or already own, them, you will unquestionably need specialist advice.

Business property

As Chapter 7 explained, investments in some types of business property qualify for relief of up to 100%. Remember that

Example: investing in business property

Mr Elephant owns assets of £900,000, made up of his house and a bank deposit. The IHT due on his estate would be £258,000. If he invested some of his assets in AIM shares instead, which qualify for 100% business property relief, then his ultimate IHT liability may be reduced as follows:

Assets	Original estate, £000	Reinvested estate, £000
AIM shares	–	250
House & contents	500	500
Bank deposit	400	150
Total estate	£900	£900
Less assets qualifying for 100% relief	Nil	(250)
Less nil-rate band	(255)	(255)
Taxable estate	£645	£395
IHT @ 40%	£258	£158
Potential tax saving		£100

this includes shares listed on the Alternative Investment Market (AIM). The benefit from investing money in business property can be seen from the example of Mr Elephant above.

EIS and VCTs

Shares in Enterprise Investment Scheme (EIS) companies qualify for business property relief. However, shares in Venture Capital Trusts (VCTs) do not. Similarly, cash and investments held in Personal Equity Plans (PEPs) and Indi-

vidual Savings Accounts (ISAs) do not qualify for any relief
from IHT.

Farms

If you own a farm this may attract agricultural property relief
at either 100% or 50%. The definition of a farm is fairly wide.
It includes farm buildings and farmhouses, together with the
land occupied with them, if they are of a character appropriate to the property. However, this area is complex and you
should take specialist advice.

The breeding and rearing of horses on a stud farm and the
grazing of horses in connection with those activities also
qualify for agricultural property relief. This includes any
buildings used in connection with those activities.

In order to get relief, you must have occupied the property
for agricultural purposes for at least two years. Alternatively,
if the property is used by somebody else for agricultural purposes, you must have owned it for seven years.

You will be entitled to agricultural property relief at 100%
if you have the right to vacant possession (or the right to
obtain vacant possession within twelve months). Otherwise,
50% relief is due.

Woodlands

The acquisition of a woodlands estate is a long-term investment (normally a minimum of ten years), but it can provide
valuable IHT savings. Woodlands can be acquired at various
stages of development and certain trees can take 50 years to

reach their full size. The work involved would normally be undertaken by professional forestry managers.

For IHT purposes, 100% of the value of the standing timber may attract relief, making it effectively tax-free provided you have owned it for two years. A commercially run woodlands investment is worth considering if you wish to pass wealth to your family in a tax-efficient manner.

Lloyd's underwriters

If you are a Lloyd's underwriter you will qualify for business property relief at 100% on all assets contained in the Lloyd's business, and also for property subject to Lloyd's deposit guarantees.

Heritage land and buildings

If you own certain heritage assets then these are exempt from IHT, provided you allow reasonable public access to them and undertake to maintain and preserve the property. The assets must also stay within the UK.

The types of asset that this exemption might apply to are:

- Works of art and other objects of national scientific, historic or artistic interest;
- Land of outstanding scenic, historic or scientific interest;
- Buildings (and objects associated with such buildings) of outstanding historic and architectural interest.

9

Trusts

TRUSTS ARE USED for a variety of reasons. Historically, this was frequently for tax avoidance purposes. However, many of the tax benefits are no longer applicable and trusts are in fact used for a variety of other reasons, for example, when you wish to pass capital down to another generation but maintain control over how much your child or grandchild has to spend. Giving the beneficiary absolute control over the assets may be considered to be too much of an invitation to spend, spend, and spend!

It is important to remember when you set up a trust that you are actually giving your assets away and that they will no longer belong to you. Some key terms in relation to trusts are set out in the table on page 70.

There are different types of trust and the suitability of the trust will depend upon the particular circumstances. As Chapter 3 explained, the transfer of assets into a trust may be either a Potentially Exempt Transfer (PET), taxable only if you die within seven years, or a chargeable lifetime transfer, in which case tax could be payable immediately.

A solicitor will be able to draw up a trust deed for you and you should consider carefully who you would like to be the

Settlor	The person who creates the trust
Trustees	The individuals who look after the assets on behalf of the beneficiaries
Beneficiaries	The persons able to benefit under the terms of the trust deed
Interest	The entitlement that a beneficiary receives from a trust. This may be an interest in the trust income for life (a 'life interest') or for a set period, or may be an interest in the capital
Trust deed	A legal document governing how the assets should be dealt with, who the beneficiaries are etc.
Letter of wishes	A letter provided to the trustees by the settlor that is not legally binding, and which explains how the settlor would like certain matters to be dealt with
Protector	The settlor may wish to appoint someone, such as a family friend, as 'protector' of the trust. A protector could keep a watchful eye over the trustees and would have certain powers, such as the ability to hire and fire trustees

trustees. You may wish to be a trustee yourself and also appoint the family accountant or solicitor. In most cases, it is necessary to register the trust with the Inland Revenue.

The Society of Trust and Estate Practitioners has some helpful information on its website (www.step.org). Additionally, the Inland Revenue website (www.inlandrevenue.gov.uk) has some useful guidance.

Types of trust

Bare trust

This is the most straightforward trust. Under a bare trust the beneficiary is entitled outright to the capital and income. They are usually used if the beneficiary is a minor and the trust funds are being held on their behalf by adult trustees until the beneficiary is old enough to give a valid receipt. For example, the opening of a bank account in your child's name is a bare trust. Once the beneficiary is over 18 years old, he or she can insist at any time that the assets be transferred into his or her name.

The transfer of the assets into the bare trust will count as a PET by you (with the associated IHT and capital gains tax consequences). The assets will then form part of the beneficiary's estate for IHT. They are therefore a useful tool for IHT planning if, for example, you wish to give cash to your grandchildren, provided you survive seven years. However, note that while your children (but not grandchildren) are under 18, you will continue to be liable to pay income tax on any income arising on gifts made by you to them, unless it is less than £100 per year per child.

Interest in possession trust

Under this type of trust, a beneficiary has a limited interest in the trust funds, such as an interest in a share of the trust income for life or for a period of years (say to age 35). After the interest comes to an end, a further interest in the income may pass to someone else or another beneficiary may become entitled to the assets.

A beneficiary who is entitled to a share of the trust income is said to have an 'interest in possession' in the trust fund. The underlying capital that gives rise to that income is treated as part of the estate of the beneficiary (see Chapter 4). The IHT liability on the assets in the trust is paid by the trustees from those assets.

The transfer of assets into the trust counts as PET. If the interest in the trust income passes from one beneficiary to another (when, say, the beneficiary reaches 35 years), that interest also counts as a PET made by the first beneficiary. However, if the beneficiary (at 35 years, say) becomes entitled to both the income and capital, and no entitlement passes to any other beneficiary, this does not count as a gift for IHT purposes, provided the beneficiary retains the assets.

An interest in possession trust is useful if you would like your child to be entitled to an income stream but not entitled to the actual capital until later on in life. For example, if a husband and wife each have children from previous marriages, they may wish to protect the other spouse during his or her lifetime but ensure that their wealth passes to their own, rather than the other spouse's, children on death. This may be achieved by settling funds in trust for the settlor during the settlor's own lifetime, his or her spouse during his or her lifetime and the settlor's children after the spouse's death. These trusts are also useful for IHT planning, as assets transferred to the trust are removed from your estate, provided you survive seven years.

Discretionary trust

This is the most flexible of all the trusts but the least attractive for IHT purposes. The settlor can leave his or her options open by gifting wealth into a trust and naming a list of beneficiaries whom he or she might like to benefit in the future. It is then the decision of the trustees as to which beneficiary can benefit and when. But a gift into a discretionary trust is the only occasion on which a charge to IHT can arise immediately during your lifetime, because it is a chargeable transfer, not a PET.

If it is possible for the gift into the trust to be kept within the nil-rate band (of £255,000 in 2003/04), then no tax will be payable. The gift will still be set against your nil-rate band for a period of seven years so it could increase the tax on the rest of your estate if you die before then. However, discretionary trusts set up under a will can be a useful way of using your nil-rate band on death. These are known as 'nil-rate discretionary will trusts' and they are discussed further in Chapter 2.

If the value of a lifetime gift to a discretionary trust exceeds the nil-rate band, and no reliefs are available to reduce this, then the settlor will pay IHT at the lifetime rate of 20% (on the excess over the nil-rate band) at the time of creating the trust and when transferring further assets into the trust at a later date.

Every ten years there is a special tax charge on the trustees of a discretionary trust. The trustees are subject to IHT on the value of the trust at that date plus any amounts paid out in the previous ten years. This total IHT, minus any available nil-rate band, is then taxed at a maximum of 6%. There may also be tax on a distribution of capital if the value of the trust at the previous ten-year point (or on commencement) was above the nil-rate band.

The tax position of discretionary trusts is complex and if you are a trustee of one or are considering setting one up, you should seek professional advice.

Accumulation and maintenance trusts

These trusts enjoy a special IHT status. They are suited to situations where grandparents make gifts into a trust for their grandchildren.

Initially the trust will be discretionary in nature, because it is set up for a pool of beneficiaries (usually the grandchildren) and income can be paid out for their maintenance at the discretion of the trustees. Any income not paid out is accumulated within the trust. However, unlike other discretionary trusts, the gift into the trust is a PET rather than a chargeable lifetime transfer and the trustees do not have a liability on distributions of capital nor on every tenth anniversary.

Beneficiaries must take an interest in the trust income and possibly capital by age 25. The share of capital will be treated as part of their estate from that point on. They will either have an interest in possession (see previously) or the funds will pass from the trust into their estate.

Other considerations

This brief summary of IHT issues relevant to trusts can only scratch the surface, and if you are considering making a trust either during your lifetime or in a will you should seek professional advice.

Each type of trust has its own income tax and capital gains tax considerations that will need to be borne in mind. Be careful to fully exclude yourself and your spouse from benefit, and if you are transferring assets into a trust for your young children, be aware that you are likely to remain subject to tax on the income and, in some circumstances, gains.

10

The overseas element

THE UK HAS OFTEN BEEN DESCRIBED as a tax haven for those coming to live here from abroad. It has a peculiar tax system that gives certain tax benefits if you are 'domiciled' outside the UK.

Most people are familiar with the rules relating to residence (i.e. where you live on a day-to-day basis), but broadly speaking domicile means where you have your long-term connections and where you consider is home (see opposite).

IHT is geared towards domicile rather than residence:

- If you are domiciled in the UK, you are subject to IHT on your worldwide assets;
- If you are domiciled overseas, you are chargeable to IHT on your UK-sited assets only.

Often the opportunity to take advantage of not being domiciled in the UK is overlooked. But with careful planning, your IHT bill can be substantially reduced. Remember, though, that if you are UK domiciled the spouse exemption is reduced to £55,000 if your spouse is non-domiciled (see page 23).

Possible reform

The Inland Revenue is reviewing the tax rules in relation to non-domiciled individuals. So now is the time for you to review your position and plan accordingly, before any changes are introduced.

What is domicile?

The term domicile is a matter of general law. Its rules are different from those of residence and should not be confused with nationality or citizenship.

When you are born, you acquire a domicile of origin, which is usually your father's domicile at the time of your birth. (This is not the case if you are illegitimate or born after your father's death, in which case you take your mother's domicile.) Your domicile then follows that of your father until the age of sixteen. A domicile of origin sticks to you like glue and it's quite hard to shake off. You will acquire a domicile of choice in the UK if you move here and intend to stay permanently or indefinitely. There are special rules for women who married before 1 January 1974.

In some cases, it may be possible to ask the Inland Revenue for a ruling on whether you count as non-domiciled. However, in most instances you would complete your Self Assessment Tax Return certifying that you consider yourself to be non-domiciled. The Inland Revenue is of course entitled to challenge your domicile position.

Deemed domicile

Even if you are not UK-domiciled, for IHT purposes you are deemed to be domiciled in the UK if you have been resident in the UK for seventeen of the last twenty years of assessment, or if you were domiciled in the UK in the three years before a chargeable transfer. These rules present certain traps for the unwary. For example, you are deemed resident for a tax year, even if you are only present in the UK for part of that year.

Example: deemed domicile

Mr Zebra moved to the UK on 4 April 1986, and has been resident here for tax purposes ever since.

He is counted as resident under these rules in the 1985/86 tax year, even though he was only here for two days. He will therefore be treated as deemed domiciled with effect from 6 April 2002.

If he had arrived two days later, he would not have been treated as deemed domiciled until 6 April 2003.

On becoming deemed domiciled, your worldwide assets become subject to UK IHT. It is therefore important that your affairs are planned properly before you become deemed domiciled.

One possible planning idea is to 'break' your deemed domicile status. This would involve you leaving the UK for four complete tax years. Return visits to the UK (within strict limits) are allowed during that period.

> **Example: breaking your deemed domicile**
> Mr Racoon became deemed domiciled on 6 April 2002. He
> decides to leave the UK on 31 March 2003 and returns on 10
> April 2007. He has broken his deemed domicile position and
> the seventeen-year clock starts again on 6 April 2007.

Basic planning

If you are not domiciled in the UK, you may still have assets
here, even after you have left the country. If you should die,
those assets remain subject to IHT. By rearranging your
wealth, substantial savings can be made.

> **Example: rearranging assets to save tax**
> Miss Armadillo is non-UK domiciled. Shortly after returning to
> her home in Sweden, she passed away, leaving the following
> UK assets.
>
> | | £ |
> |---|---:|
> | UK property | 230,000 |
> | UK bank deposit | 180,000 |
> | UK quoted shares | 100,000 |
> | Total UK estate | £510,000 |
> | IHT on: £255,000 (the nil-rate band) | Nil |
> | £255,001–£510,000 @ 40% | 102,000 |
>
> This IHT liability could easily have been avoided by
> transferring the UK bank deposit to an overseas account,
> selling some of the UK quoted shares and reinvesting in
> overseas securities (subject to commercial considerations, of
> course!).

The use of trusts

The use of trusts is of particular importance if you are non-UK domiciled. This is because any overseas assets you transfer into an offshore trust are excluded from charge to IHT, even if you subsequently become deemed domiciled in the UK. However, this rule is currently under consideration by the Inland Revenue.

Example: using an offshore trust

Mr Wallaby is domiciled in Australia. He will become deemed domiciled for IHT purposes on 6 April 2004. He has overseas assets of £4m. Before 6 April 2004, Mr Wallaby settles an offshore trust and transfers those assets to it. The assets then remain outside the UK IHT net, even when Mr Wallaby becomes deemed domiciled.

Obviously the income tax and capital gains tax implications also need to be considered.

Useful information

IHT rates 2003/04

On death	*Rate of tax*
£0 – £255,000	Nil
Over £255,000	40%

During lifetime	*Rate of tax*
(i.e. on transfers to a discretionary trust)	
£0 – £255,000	Nil
Over £255,000	20%

Taper relief for lifetime gifts

Period between transfer and death	*Rate of reduction in tax liability*
0–3 years	0%
3–4 years	20%
4–5 years	40%
5–6 years	60%
6–7 years	80%

Inland Revenue leaflets

IHT2	'Inheritance Tax on lifetime gifts'
IHT3	'Inheritance Tax. An introduction'
IHT12	'Inheritance Tax. When is an Excepted Estate Grant appropriate?'
IHT12(S)	'Inheritance Tax. When is an Excepted Estate Grant appropriate?' (The rules in Scotland)
IHT14	'Inheritance Tax. The personal representatives' responsibilities'
IR45	'What to do about tax when someone dies'
IR152	'Trusts. An introduction'

Addresses and websites

BDO Stoy Hayward
8 Baker Street
London W1U 3LL
Telephone: 0870 567 5678
Fax: 020 7487 3686
www.bdo.co.uk

The Chartered Institute of Taxation
12 Upper Belgrave Street
London SW1X 8BB
Telephone: 020 7235 9381
Fax: 020 7235 2562
www.tax.org.uk

The Society of Trust and Estate Tax Practitioners
26 Dover Street
London W1S 4LY
Telephone: 020 7763 7152
Fax: 020 7763 7252
www.step.org

Inland Revenue (Probate and IHT helpline)
Telephone: 0845 302 0900
www.inlandrevenue.gov.uk

Acknowledgements

I WOULD LIKE TO THANK many people for their help. Peter Raddenbury, Charles Pascoe and Laura Merrigan helped and encouraged me with the writing of this book. Lee Knight and Simon Davis assisted with some of the chapters. Rahema Alibaba and Jane Hill typed the manuscript. Andrew Franklin at Profile Books, my publisher, was invaluable. And I would like to thank Jane Vass, who helped enormously with getting the book into its final form.

Finally, thanks to Justin and my parents for their continuous support and encouragement. Also to my children Gemma and Alex, who just want to see their names in print!

Current and forthcoming BDO titles

Finance Directors
A BDO Stoy Hayward Guide for Growing Businesses
by Rupert Merson

What is the role of the finance director in a smaller or
medium-sized business with ambitions to grow? And what is
the experience of working as a finance director in an entrepre-
neurial environment actually like?

Rupert Merson's entertaining, informative and up-to-date
guide is intended for both the entrepreneur and the potential
finance director. Straightforward and practical, it is the essential introduction to the subject.

ISBN 1 86197 454 X

£6.99

Non-executive Directors
A BDO Stoy Hayward Guide for Growing Businesses
by Rupert Merson

The role of the non-executive director has never before come under such scrutiny. From once being seen as 'about as useful as Christmas tree decorations', non-executives are now seen as critical components in the corporate governance framework, and important contributors to the strategic health of companies.

Rupert Merson explores the particular contribution the non-executive can make in the younger, growing, owner-managed business.

ISBN 1 86197 499 X

£6.99

Managing Directors
A BDO Stoy Hayward Guide for Growing Businesses
by Rupert Merson

Part inventor, part entrepreneur, part manager, part accountant, part leader, part salesman, part bottle-washer – the role of managing director in the younger, growing business is one of the most demanding jobs in commerce today. Yet it is surprisingly little written about. Rupert Merson plugs the gap with another of his insightful, irreverent, but as always informative guides.

ISBN 1 86197 740 9

£6.99

Owners
A BDO Stoy Hayward Guide for Growing Businesses
by Rupert Merson

The three key barriers to growth in any business with ambitions to grow are easy to identify: owners, owner-managers and managers. More's the pity that owners at least are little written about and less understood. Rupert Merson, in the next in his series on the key roles at the top of the growing business, explores perhaps the most important role of all.

ISBN 1 86197 682 8

£6.99

An Inspector Returns
The A–Z to surviving a tax investigation
by Daniel Dover & Tim Hindle
with cartoons by Michael Heath

Revised and updated second edition

If you are the subject of a tax investigation by the Inland Revenue, do not panic – read this book instead. An investigation undoubtedly means trouble, but the straightforward advice in these pages should help steer you around the worst pitfalls and survive the process intact.

'An amusing guide through this difficult subject ... This disarmingly honest little book could save you many sleepless nights.' *The Times*

ISBN 1 86197 420 5

£6.99

War or Peace
Skirmishes with the Revenue
by Daniel Dover & Tim Hindle
with cartoons by McLachlan

Each year over 250,000 people are subject to Inland Revenue enquiries. It is not a pleasant experience. But help is at hand. For the first time here is a book that explains the whole process, along with numerous tips on how to proceed and what to do – or not to do. Deftly written with wit and humour, this could save you time, misery and money.

'This is a terrific book … It is informative, easy to understand and comforting. Full marks.' *The Tax Journal*

ISBN 1 86197 524 4

£6.99